TABLE OF CONTENTS

Shortfin Mako Sharks

Sicklefin Lemon Shark

Silky Shark

Smooth Hammerhead

Speartooth Shark

Spinner Shark

Spiny Dogfish

Spotted Wobbegong

Starry Smooth-hound

Striped Catshark

Tasselled Wobbegong

Tawny Nurse Shark

Tiger Shark

Whale Shark

Whitespotted Bamboo Shark

Whitetip Reef Shark

Angel Shark

Angel Sharks are sometimes called monkfish. They are sharks with a flattened body that can grow up to 5 feet long and weigh 77 pounds. Angel Sharks also have broad fins near their head. They almost look like rays. They can be found on the sandy seabed of the waters of Morocco, Canary Islands, Norway, Sweden Mediterranean and Black Seas at a depth of 150 meters. Because of the overfishing of this shark it is considered to be critically endangered.

Australian Swellshark

Australian Swellsharks are also called draughtboard sharks. They usually measure 1 meter long. They have a stout body and a broad head. They also have a short tail. Australian Swellsharks have brown or gray patches on their skin. Australian Swellsharks can be found inhabiting rocky reef or seaweed beds at a depth of 220 meters of the waters of Australia and Tasmania. They are called swell sharks because they inflate their bodies by taking in much water and air to intimidate their enemies when threatened.

Banded Wobbegong

Banded Wobbegongs are also called Gulf Wobbegong. They can be found in the clear waters of Southern Australia at a depth of 50 meters. Banded Wobbegong have a large head and flat golden-brown body with blue gray spots that can grow up to 2.9 meters long. Their mouth has skin flaps which look like a beard from which it got its name from an Aboriginal Australian word that means "shaggy beard." They also look almost the same as Ornate Wobbegong but Banded Wobbegongs are larger in size.

Basking Shark

Basking Sharks are the **second largest living fish in the world** since they can grow up to 7.9 meters or 26 feet. Basking Sharks are grayish-brown in color and have a mottled skin. They also have an extremely enlarged, conical mouth and feed on plankton. Basking Sharks are source for food, shark liver oil, animal feed and shark fin. They can be found worldwide at 910 meter feet but overhunting on some parts of the world lead to their disappearance on some areas.

Blacktip Reef Shark

Blacktip Reef Sharks are sharks with black tips on their fins and has a strongly built streamlined brown tan body with rounded mouth and large eyes. They prefer the shallow waters of subtropical and tropical Indo-Pacific and Indian Ocean. They usually feed on sea snakes, seabirds and small bony fish. Blacktip Reef Sharks don't typically pose a danger to humans. They are also used for their meat, fins and liver oils.

Blacktip Shark

Blacktip Sharks are sharks with a stout, streamlined body that are gray above and white below. They can grow up to 1.5 meter. Blacktip Sharks have small eyes, pointed snout and black tips on their fins. But some larger Blacktip Sharks have unmarked or almost unmarked fins. They can be found swimming the tropical and subtropical waters all over the world at a depth of 30 meters.

Blind Shark

Blind Sharks are usually seen along the coast of eastern Australia at a depth of 110 meters. Their head is flat and wide with their eyes on top of it. Their top bodies are brown to black in color while their undersides are yellow in color. They usually eat small bony and non-bony fish. Blind Sharks are more active at night and can grow up to 1.2 meters. They are called blind sharks because when removed from the waters they would retract its eyeballs and shut its lower eyelids.

Blotched Catshark

Blotched Catsharks are a type of catsharks with a wide head, cat-shaped eyes and broad body. They have dark markings on their back. They also have small spots on their body that glow yellow under a blue light. Blotched Catsharks are not dangerous to humans and can be found in the waters of North Carolina, Florida, Bahamas, Cayman Island, Jamaica and the Gulf of Mexico at a depth of 329–548 meters.

Blue Shark

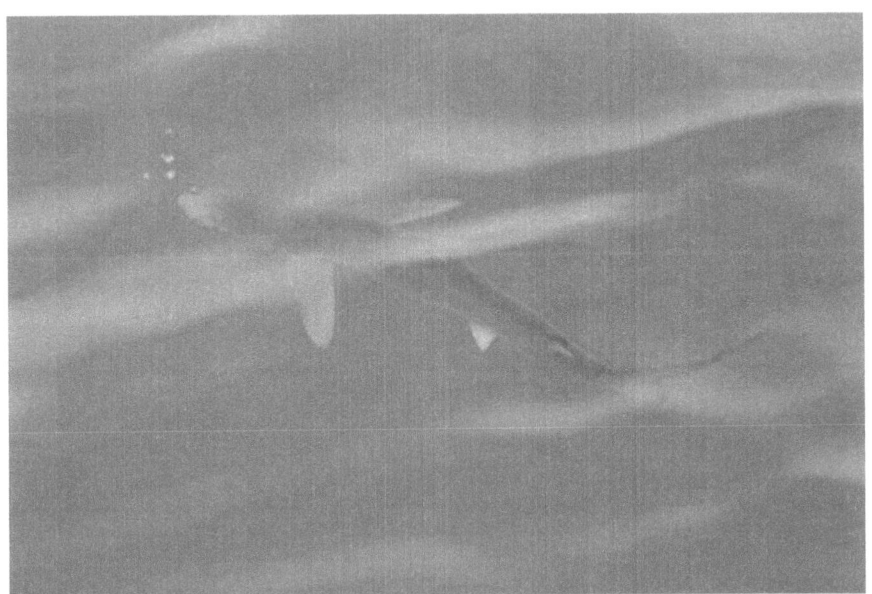

Blue Sharks live in the deep temperate and tropical waters at a depth of 350 meters. They prefer cooler waters and migrate long distances. **Blue Sharks have a deep blue color** on top of their long and slender bodies and their undersides are white in color and can grow up to 2.82 meters in length. They can also move really quickly. Their diet includes small fish and squids. They can also eat larger prey.

Bonnethead Shark

Bonnethead Sharks are also known as shovelheads. Among all the hammerhead sharks, they are the smallest hammerheads as they grow to only 3 feet. Hammerhead sharks have flattened head that are laterally extended. But the head of the Bonnethead Sharks are more rounded than the other types of Hammerhead sharks making it look like a shovel. The bodies of Bonnethead Sharks are gray-brown color above and a lighter color on the underside. They are also timid, harmless and swim in groups of 5 or 12 individuals. Bonnethead Sharks prefer to live in the sandy bottoms and coral reefs of the tropical and subtropical waters of the Gulf of Mexico, Carribean, Southern California to Ecuador, and North Carolina to Brazil at the depth of 25 to 30 meters.

Brownbanded Bamboo Shark

The Brownbanded Bamboo Sharks are also called Cat Sharks because they have a whisker like sensory organ near their mouth called a barbel. They can be seen in the waters of Japan to northern Australia at a depth of 85 meters. The adults have a brownish color overall with very faint bands on their bodies that can grow up to 1.04 meters. Young Brownbanded Bamboo Sharks on the other hand have distinctive dark and pale bands. Their numbers are near threatened because they are often hunted as food and as pets for aquarium. Did you know that they can stay out of the waters for twelve hours since they are often found near tide pools?

Bull Shark

Bull Sharks are also known as Zambezi Sharks, or Zambi in Africa. While in Nicaragua, they are called Nicaragua Sharks. They are usually found in warm and shallow salt water and even fresh water around the world at a depth of 150 meters. They are also aggressive and are responsible for most near-shore shark attacks. The color of their stout body ranges from light to dark gray color on top and having a white underside.

Chain Catshark

Chain Catsharks are also known as chain dogfishes because of the beautiful spiderwebbing on its yellowish brown body. They are small sharks that can grow at only 1.94 feet. Chain Catsharks are harmless and are rarely encountered by humans as they prefer the Caribbean Sea, the Gulf of Mexico, northwest and western Atlantic Ocean and the waters of the continental shelf of northeastern United States at a depth of 36 to 750 meters and usually feed on squid and bony fish. During daytime, Chain Catsharks rest at the bottom of the water.

Cookiecutter Shark

Cookiecutter Sharks are also known as cigar sharks. They can be found in warm, oceanic waters all over the world at the depth of 3.7 kilometers. Cookiecutter Sharks have a long, cylinder-shaped body that only grow up to 1.87 feet. They also have a short snout and teeth like a saw thus the name given to them. Their bodies are grayish brown in color on top and a lighter color on their underside.

Coral Catshark

Coral Catsharks are found on shallow coral reefs across the Indo-West Pacific at a depth of 15 meters. They have a slender body and short head. Coral Catsharks also have black and white spots all over their body that grow only up to 2.29 feet. Just like all sharks, they are mainly inactive at day and only search for food at night.

Crested Bullhead Shark

Crested Bullhead Sharks are an uncommon type of bullhead sharks that inhabit the coast of eastern Australia. They are often found at the depth of 93 meters. Crested Bullhead Sharks can grow up to 3.9 feet and have dark blotches on their light brown to yellow-brown body. They also have ridges above their eyes. Crested Bullhead Sharks hunt sea urchins and other small organisms for food.

Dusky Whaler

Dusky Sharks are found in tropical and warm seas at a depth of 450 meters. They are large sharks reaching up to 14 feet in length that have brown or bluish-grey top body and white underside. Their snouts are short and round. They eat a variety of food, including bony fish, rays, sharks, sea turtles, marine mammals and garbage.

Dwarf Sawfish

Dwarf Sawfish are also called Queensland Sawfish. They are called Dwarf Sawfish because it is the smallest among the types of Sawfish. Dwarf Sawfish are considered endangered because of overhunting for their oil and meat. They're usually found in the tropical water of Australia at the depth of 10 meters. Their body is olive brown in color that can grow up to 10 feet and shaped like a torpedo. Dwarf Sawfish has a snout that is flat and elongated, with about twenty pairs of teeth.

Epaulette Shark

Epaulette Sharks are a type of long-tailed carpet shark. Carpet Sharks are types of sharks that have intricate patterns on their bodies. They can be seen in the tropical waters of New Guinea and Australia at a depth of 50 meters. They have large black spots near their head. These spots are bordered with white. Epaulette Sharks can grow up to 3.3 feet only. They can "walk" on water, by wriggling their bodies and pushing with their paired fins.

Freshwater Sawfish

Freshwater Sawfish are also called largetooth sawfish and Leichhardt's Sawfish. They can grow up to 7 meters long. Freshwater Sawfish have a heavy body. They also have a snout with a short massive saw: This saw has large teeth on each side, usually around 14 to 22 teeth. They are called Freshwater Sawfish because they can be found not only in the tropical and subtropical saltwater but are also known to enter freshwater as well.

Frilled Shark

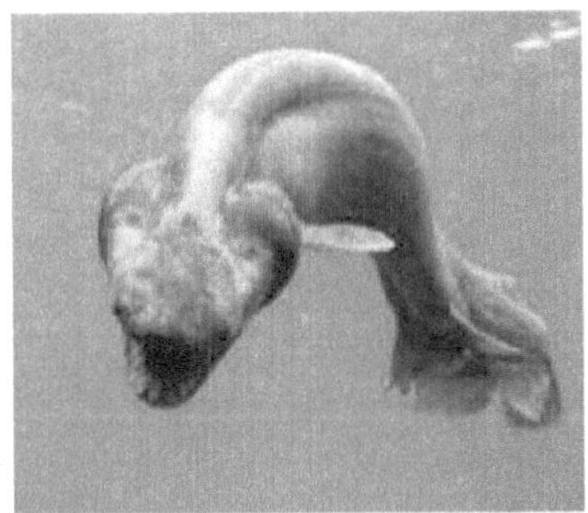

Frilled Sharks are found throughout the Atlantic and Pacific Oceans at the depth of 50 to 200 meters. They can reach 2 meters in length. They also have a body that resembles an eel. Frilled sharks are dark brown in color and their six pairs of gill slits look like frills.

Galapagos Bullhead Shark

Galapagos Bullhead Sharks are found in the Eastern Pacific Ocean at the depth of 3 to 40 meters. They are also known as the Peruvian Horn Shark. Bullhead Sharks are sharks that have a short but blunt head with high ridges just above their eyes. Galapagos Bullhead Sharks have dark spots on their brownish skin. With the help of the large fins near their head, they are able to crawl on ocean floors. They can grow up to 1.07 meters.

Galapagos Shark

Galapagos Sharks are found worldwide. They can grow up to 3 meters and are also dangerous and aggressive towards humans. The fin on their back is tall and has a rounded tip. Their bodies are brownish gray on top with a white underside. They mainly feed on bony fish, other sharks, sea lions and garbage.

Goblin Shark

Goblin Sharks are a rare type of deep-sea shark that can be found worldwide at a depth of 1500 meters. Their snout is long and flat. They also have teeth that look like nails. Goblin Sharks can grow up to 4 meters or even larger and have a body that is pinkish gray in color. They look scary, isn't it?

Great Hammerhead Shark

Great Hammerhead Sharks are the largest type of hammerhead sharks. They can grow up to 6.1 meters. Great Hammerhead Sharks can be found worldwide at the depth of between 1 to 80 meters. Their heads resemble a wide hammer with an almost straight front. Great Hammerhead Sharks are grayish brown on top with white underside. They eat bony fish and small sharks. They are dangerous but rarely attack humans.

Great White Shark

Great White Sharks have different names such as: great white, white pointer, white shark or white death. They are very large sharks growing up to 6 meters and even over 8 meters in length making it the **largest predatory fish**. Great White Sharks have bodies that are dark gray on top and an all-white underside. Their estimated life span is 70 years or more. They can be found in the east and west US coast, the golf coast, South America, Australia, New Zealand, Hawaii, the Mediterranean Sea, West Africa, Japan and East China. They also have the most number of recorded attacks on humans.

Green Sawfish

The Green Sawfish is also called the longcomb sawfish. They can grow up to 7.3 meters in length and are considered the largest of all the sawfishes. Their bodies are typical for a shark but have a blade-like, elongated snout. This snout has teeth on each side that look like a saw. They are called Green Sawfish because they have bodies that are greenish brown on top and a white underside. Green Sawfish can be found in only small numbers and are considered endangered because of the continuous destruction of their habitat. They can be found at the subtropical and tropical waters of the Indo Pacific Ocean.

Greenland Shark

Greenland Sharks are also called gurry sharks or grey sharks. They can be found in the cold waters around Canada, Greenland, Norway and Iceland. Female Greenland Sharks are typically larger than males and can grow up to 7 meters. Greenland Sharks are slow swimmers. They are **one of the slowest swimming sharks** at a speed of 0.3 m/s. Their top bodies may have brown, gray or black color and can also have white spots and dark lines. They have the most toxic meat of all sharks. But did you know that in Iceland they would treat the meat of this shark to reduce its toxin and eat is as a delicacy?

Grey Bamboo Shark

The Grey Bamboo Shark is a type of carpet shark that can be found in the waters of the Indo Pacific Ocean. Their length is up to 74 cm. Adult Grey Bamboo Sharks are brown without any other coloration. Young Grey Bamboo Sharks, on the other hand, have dark bands.

Grey Nurse Shark

Grey Nurse Sharks are also called as spotted ragged-tooth sharks, sand tiger sharks, or blue-nurse sand tigers. They usually live in the waters of Australia, South Africa, Japan, Mediterranean and east coasts of South and North America at the depth of 191 meters. Grey Nurse Sharks as their name suggest has a grey to grey-brown color on top and with white belly. They can grow up to 1.9 meters. Grey Nurse Sharks move slowly. They do not attack humans.

Grey Reef Shark

Grey Reef Sharks are fast swimmers. When hunting for their food, they can swim at a speed of 25 miles per hour. They have large eyes. They also have a broad and rounded snout. Their body has a plain or white tip on the fin on their back, and dark tips on the other fins Grey Reefs Sharks are grey on top of their body and have a white underside. They feed primarily on bony fish. They are reef sharks commonly found around the shallow waters near the drop-offs of the coral reefs of the Indian and Pacific Oceans in depths less than 60 meters.

Horn Shark

The Horn Shark is a type of bullhead shark. They are small sharks, measuring only up to 1 meter in length. Horn Sharks are brown or gray in color. It got its name because of its short but blunt head that has high ridges just above the eyes. They also have numerous small dark spots on their body. Horn Sharks usually hunt food at night. They inhabit the warm waters of the western North America.

Japanese Bullhead Shark

Japanese Bullhead Sharks are commonly found in the northwestern Pacific Ocean in depths of 6 to 37 meters. They frequent the kelp beds or the rocky bottom of the ocean. Japanese Bullhead Sharks have a short but blunt head and two high fins on their back. They also have irregular vertical brown bands and stripes on their body. Japanese Bullhead Sharks can grow up to 1.3 meters in length.

Lemon Shark

Lemon Sharks are bulky and powerful sharks with yellowish brown skin color thus the name given to them. They can grow up to 3 meters long and inhabit the coastal inshore waters of New Jersey in the USA to Southern Brazil in the tropical western Atlantic Ocean. Lemon Sharks have a flat head with broad and short snout. They are nocturnal predators that mostly hunt for fish.

Leopard Shark

The Leopard Shark is a type of houndshark. They have a long and slender body with black markings and large dark spots on their back thus the name given to them. Lemon Sharks can grow up to 1.5 meters. They are harmless to humans and are commonly caught by fisheries as they commonly inhabit bays, estuaries and areas near the coast at depths of 4 meters.

Lesser-spotted Catshark

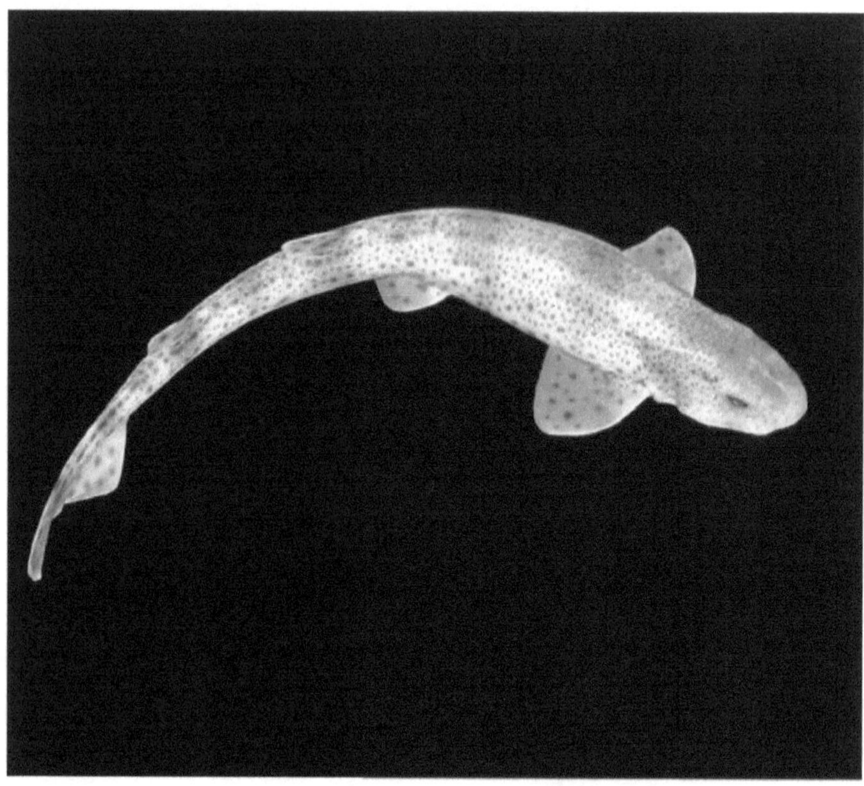

Lesser-spotted Catsharks are also known as small-spotted catsharks, rough-hound or morgay. They can grow up to 1 meter long and have a blunt head. Their nostrils are under their snout and their skin is rough like sandpaper. They have a slender body that is grayish-brown on top with brown spots and white underside. Lesser-spotted Catsharks can be found in the waters of Norway and British Isles to Mediterranean, Senegal and the Ivory Coast.

Necklace Carpetshark

Necklace Carpetsharks are sharks found in Australian Waters at depths of 150 meter. They frequent the kelp and sea beds as well as the coral reefs. Necklace Carpetsharks have a long tube-like body and small fins. Their snout is short and rounded. They are light brown or dark brown in color with a broad collar of beautiful white spots over their gills that look like a necklace. Necklace Carpetsharks can grow up to 3 feet.

Nurse Shark

Nurse Sharks can reach a length of up to 10.1 feet. They have rounded fins, a broad head, and are brownish in color. Nurse Sharks are mainly active at night and hide during daytime. It is unclear how they got their name but it might probably because of the sucking sound they made when they look for their prey which is the same as the sound of a nursing baby. They are bottom dwelling sharks that inhabit the waters of the Caribbean Islands.

Nursehound

Nursehounds are also called large-spotted dogfish, greater spotted dogfish or bull huss. They have a broad and rounded head with stout bodies that tapers toward the tail. They are closely related and are almost similar to Lesser-spotted Catsharks. They are also active at night and hide in small holes during the day and can be seen in the waters of northeastern Atlantis, Canary Islands and Mediterranean Sea at the depth of 20 to 60 meters.

Oceanic Whitetip Shark

Oceanic Whitetip Sharks are also called brown shark, silvertip shark and oceanic white-tipped whaler. They have a sturdily built body with long and rounded fins. These fins have a white or silvery tip. The color of the top of the Oceanic Whitetip Sharks varies; it can be brown, bluish or greyish in color but the underside is always white. Oceanic Whitetip Sharks can grow up to 4 meters and are widely distributed worldwide. They are aggressive and dangerous to shipwreck or air crash survivors. The numbers of the Oceanic Whitetip Sharks are swiftly dwindling in numbers due to overfishing. Their fins are heavily traded.

Ornate Wobbegong

The Ornate Wobbegong is a type of carpet shark. They have a stocky body, flat head and a stout tail. Ornate Wobbegongs have a fringe along the front of their face like a beard. Their skin is also used for leather. When harassed or attacked, they may bite humans. Ornate Wobbegong can grow up to 2.5 meters. They can be found near coral reefs and algal covered rocky areas of the tropical waters of the Indo-Pacific Region.

Pelagic Thresher

Pelagic Thresher is a type of Thresher Shark. Thresher Sharks can be identified because the upper lobe (caudal fin) of their tail is long and whip like. Pelagic Threshers are also the smallest among the Thresher Sharks. They usually measure around 3 meters long and have coppery brown color on top of their body and a white underside. Pelagic Thresher Sharks can be found in the Indian and Pacific Oceans. Their numbers are also greatly declining in numbers

Pocket Shark

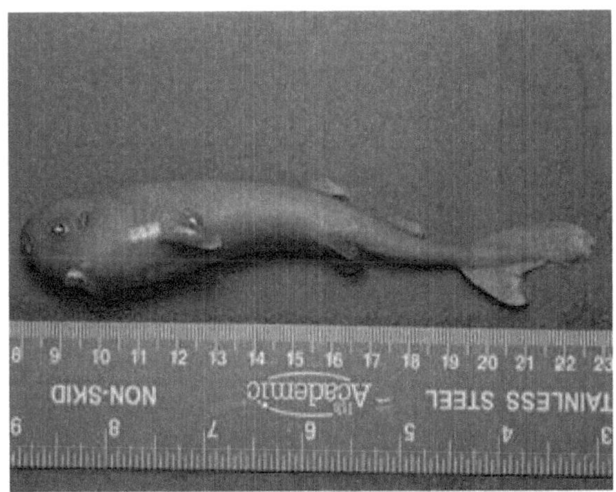

Pocket Sharks are a type of kitefin shark. They are usually found in the deep waters of Chile. Near their front fins, they have two large pockets with no known purpose. Pocket Sharks have blunt heads, round snouts and cigar-shaped bodies that grow to only about 5.5 inches. There's isn't much available information about them. They are considered the **rarest of all sharks**.

Port Jackson Shark

Port Jackson Sharks are a type of bullhead shark. They are found in the coasts of southern Australia. They have a blunt but large head. They also have a light brown body with dark brown markings. Port Jackson Sharks usually grow up to 5.5 ft. long.

Puffadder Shyshark

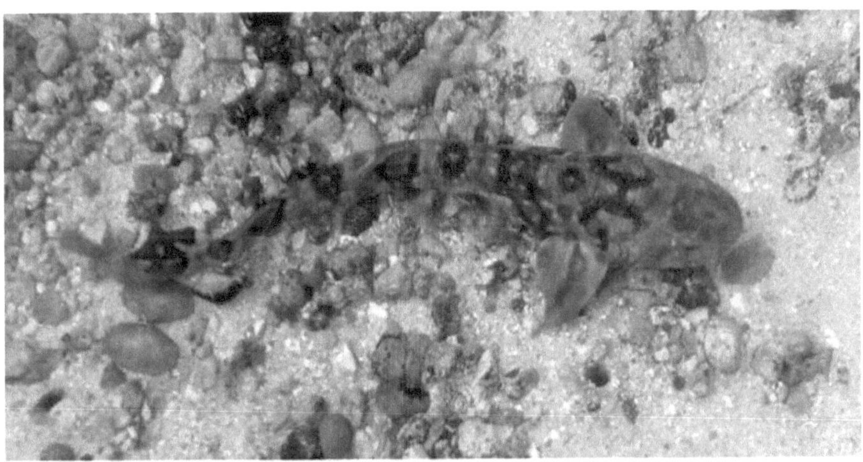

Puffadder Shysharks are also known as Happy Eddie. They have a flattened body and head. Puffadder Shysharks have dark, orange and white markings on their body that can grow only up to 2 feet. When threatened, they usually curl into a circle, their tail covering their eyes thus earning the name "shyshark."

Sandbar Shark

Sandbar Sharks are native to the Atlantic Ocean and the Indo-Pacific and inhabit the muddy or sandy bottoms of the shallow coastal waters. They are also known as thickskin sharks and brown sharks. Sandbar Sharks have a tall fin on their back. Their snout is also shorter compared to other sharks' snouts. Sandbar Sharks have a stocky body that is bluish grey or brown to bronze on top with a white underside.

Scalloped Hammerhead

Scalloped Hammerheads are also called bronze, kidney headed or southern hammerheads. They are fairly large in size and can grow up to 5.9 feet. Their eyes and nostrils are at the tips of their hammer-shaped head that have indentions on it thus the name given to them. Scalloped Hammerheads have light grey or bronzy color on top of their body and a white underside. Because of overfishing, their numbers are declining thus they were considered to be an endangered species.

Shortfin Mako Sharks

Shortfin Mako Sharks are also called blue pointers because they have a pointed snout and a metallic bluish colored body on top and a white underside. They are a large type of mackerel shark (they prefer to prey on mackerel), reaching up to 10 feet long. Together with the Longfin Mako Shark, they are commonly referred to as the Mako Sharks. Did you know that they are the **fastest swimming shark**? They can swim at 42 miles per hour and inhabits the offshore waters of tropical and temperate oceans around the world.

Sicklefin Lemon Shark

Sicklefin Lemon Sharks are also called sharptooth lemon sharks. They are closely related to lemon sharks. They are also slow-moving sharks that have a blunt head and sickle-shaped fins. Sickle Lemon Sharks have a yellowish body on top with a white underside and can grow up to 3.8 meters. They usually feed on bony fish. They are potentially dangerous but usually retreat when approached.

Silky Shark

Silky Sharks are also known as olive shark, sickle shark, blackspot shark or grey whaler shark. They can be found in tropical waters around the world. The texture of their skin is smooth thus the name given to them. Their color is grayish-bronze above their body and white below. They can grow to about 2.5 meters in length.

Smooth Hammerhead

The Smooth Hammerhead is the second largest hammerhead shark as they can grow up to 5 meters. Their hammerhead shaped head have no indentations on it thus the name given to them. They're usually found worldwide. Their main foods are bony and non-bony fish, sharks and rays. Smooth Hammerhead Sharks are captured and used in making shark fin soup. They are also dangerous and are responsible for some attacks on humans.

Speartooth Shark

Speartooth Sharks are extremely rare. They can only be found in fast-moving waters. Speartooth Sharks are gray in color and have a stocky built. They also have tiny eyes and a short snout. Speartooth Sharks have large, triangular upper teeth and narrow, spear-like lower teeth thus the name given to them. They can grow up to 2.6 meters. Sadly, it is estimated that they are about only 2500 Speartooth Sharks around the world and thus it is considered as an endangered species.

Spinner Shark

Spinner Sharks are interesting sharks. As a feeding strategy, they perform spinning leaps. They look like a larger version of Blacktip Sharks. Their maximum length is 3 meters. Spinner Sharks have a pointed snout and a slim body. They are not dangerous to humans. They can be found in warm temperate and tropical waters around the world except in the eastern Pacific Ocean.

Spiny Dogfish

Spiny Dogfish are also called spurdog, piked dogfish and mud shark. They are one of the best-known members of the dogfish family. The name dogfish was given to them because they were known to chase their prey in group or in dog-pack. They have two spines or fins, on their back. Their bodies are grey in color with white spots on top and a white underside. Spiny Dogfish are small sharks that can grow to only 39 inches. They are found in waters in most parts of the world.

Spotted Wobbegong

Spotted Wobbegongs are found in the eastern Indian Ocean. They usually grow up to 3 meters long. They also have a flattened head and body. Spotted Wobbegongs are yellow-green or brown in color with O-shaped markings on their body.

Starry Smooth-hound

Starry Smooth-hound is a type of houndshark. They can grow up to 1.4 meters long. Their lean bodies are gray or grayish-brown with white spots on top. Their undersides are pure white. They inhabit the Mediterranean Sea and the eastern Atlantic Ocean at the depth of 200 meters.

Striped Catshark

Striped Catsharks are also called pyjama sharks. They have a very unique appearance: They have thick, dark stripes running along their stocky body. Striped Catsharks are mainly active at night. During most of the day, they just lay motionless and hidden. They can grow up to 1.1 meter and can be found only in the coastal waters of South Africa.

Tasselled Wobbegong

Tasselled Wobbegongs have a fringe around their head. They often grow up to 1.8 meters long. Their body and head are broad and flattened with a complex pattern of blotches and reticulations. During the day, they just lay and rest. When night comes they actively look for food. They can be found living in the coral reefs of New Guinea, Australia and the islands near it.

Tawny Nurse Shark

Tawny Nurse Sharks are usually found in the coastlines of the Indo-Pacific Region. They prefer shallow waters. Tawny Nurse Sharks have a body shaped like a cylinder and can grow up to 3.2 meters. Their head is broad and flat. They have a similar appearance to Nurse Sharks.

Tiger Shark

Tiger Sharks are commonly known as Sea Tigers. They are large and can grow up to 5 meters long. They have dark stripes on their body; which are similar to a tiger's. Tiger Sharks usually hunt food at night. Their diet includes fish, seals, birds, turtles, sea snakes, dolphins and smaller sharks. They are second to the Great White Shark when it comes to the most number of fatal attacks to humans. They can be found inhabiting subtropical and tropical waters around the world.

Whale Shark

Whale Sharks are the **largest known living fish**. They can grow up to 12.65 meters long. They are also slow-moving carpet sharks that have a bluish gray or brown black color with white spots and pale horizontal and vertical lines on top and a white underside. Whale Sharks can be seen in the open waters of tropical oceans. They have very large mouths and feed only on plankton. Despite their big size, they don't pose threat to humans as they only feed on planktons and small fishes. Their numbers are dwindling and are considered an endangered species.

Whitespotted Bamboo Shark

Whitespotted Bamboo Sharks are small. They can grow up to only 1 meter long. Whitespotted Bamboo Sharks are mainly active at night and can be found in the Indo-West Pacific Ocean. They have a light brownish to grayish body with dark brown stripes and white spots. Whitespotted Bambook Sharks are also harmless to humans and are occasionally kept as pets at home in larger aquariums.

Whitetip Reef Shark

Whitetip Reef Sharks are small sharks. They do not grow longer than 1.6 meters. Whitetip Reef Sharks have a short and broad head, and a slender body. Their eyes are oval with vertical pupils. It got its name because of their white-tipped dorsal and tail fins. They are rarely aggressive towards humans. Whitetip Reef Sharks inhabits the Indo-Pacific waters and can be found at a depth between 8 to 40 meters.

Zebra Shark

Adult Zebra Sharks have a distinctive appearance. They have five long ridges running along their body and darks spots on their pale-colored body. Young Zebra Sharks have a different pattern; they have light vertical stripes on a brown background. They can grow up to 8 feet. Zebra Sharks inhabit the tropical Indo-Pacific Oceans at a depth of 62 meter.